# *The* TRUE GIFTS *of* CHRISTMAS

## Unwrapping the Meaning Behind Our Most Cherished Traditions

MEGAN ALEXANDER

LOYOLA PRESS.

LOYOLA PRESS.



COVER ART: Anastasiia Krivenok/Moment/Getty Images, MOMOKO SAKAI/iStock/Getty Images, Electric_Crayon/iStock/Getty Images Author photo: Kristy Belcher
EDITOR: Gary Jansen
BOOK DESIGN: Jill Arena and Carrie Schuler

The recipes in this book were provided by the author. Neither the author nor the publisher is responsible for individual dietary restrictions, allergies, or any adverse reactions resulting from following or modifying these recipes. Please consult a healthcare professional if you have dietary concerns.

ISBN: 978-0-8294-5897-8
Library of Congress Control Number: 2024952219

Published in Chicago, IL
Printed in China
25 26 27 28 29 30 31 32 33 34 DC 10 9 8 7 6 5 4 3 2 1

*Dedicated to my family,*
*Brian, Chace, Catcher, and Capri,*
*who are my ultimate Christmas gifts*

*To my parents Richard and Mary Shrader,*
*who instilled in me the real reason for the Season*

*To Tony Rossi and Gary Jansen,*
*who caught the vision of this book early*

*To the good folks at Loyola Press*
*who made this book possible*

*And to my real-life hero,*
*Saint Nicholas*

# LETTER TO MY READERS

Dear Reader,

I've always loved Christmas. I can still remember when, as a young girl, I watched *The Nutcracker* for the first time. I was mesmerized by the beginning of the ballet, when the curtain comes up to reveal a magical Christmas Eve party. The giant Christmas tree, the costumes, the bright colors, and the music combined to make a huge impact on me.

I also loved participating in the nativity play at my church. I was so proud to have the role of the angel Gabriel, dressed in a white sheet from our bedding stash. It was very exciting to make a grand entrance and tell Mary, "Greetings, favored one! The Lord is with you" (Luke 1:28) and then watch the story of Jesus's birth unfold. I always squealed at the first sight of Christmas decorations when they appeared in stores heralding the holiday season.

I'm a grown woman now, but the thrill of Christmas cheer still hasn't worn off. On my wedding day, I walked down the aisle to music from *The Nutcracker*. Every year, I start putting up Christmas decorations around our family's home in late August when the summer sun is still hot and the leaves haven't even begun to turn. And while some people are annoyed by Christmas music before Thanksgiving, I play holiday tunes all year. In my mind, there's nothing more beautiful and magical than sitting in a church on Christmas Eve, the space aglow with candles, as the choir sings "Silent Night."

Family Christmas

The Nutcracker

As a mother of three young children, I am aware of the uphill battle we face to keep Christmas from becoming a purely commercial, consumeristic event. Many holiday events I attend seem to revolve around noise and distractions, but they devote little time to the essence of Christmas and to the meanings behind why we do what we do at Christmastime.

It's easy to become so overwhelmed by the gifts *on* Christmas that we lose sight of the gifts *of* Christmas.

My Christmas-loving heart has felt burdened by this cultural numbing to the gifts of Christmas for years, so I finally decided to do something about it. I took my love of the holiday season into my professional life by creating a holiday television show called *Small Town Christmas*. I travel the country in search of small towns that bring Christmas to life, and each episode features their unique styles of celebrating the season. It's a joy and a blessing to see how small towns in America bring magic and meaning into the lives of people in their hometown. Some of the research for this book was done in conjunction with the filming of the show. My children's book, *The Magic of a Small Town Christmas*, is an organic offshoot of this work. And I am happy to share that I have been busy filming an upcoming movie that further reflects the best thing about Christmas. Christmas, it seems, is in everything I do!

In my work, I can't help but notice how rich with historical significance so many of our Christmas symbols and stories are. So I decided to connect the dots between the traditions and symbols of my favorite holiday and their spiritual roots. I dug through piles of history

Megan's family

Santa and Megan

books and magazine articles about the wreaths and mistletoe, cookies and candies, ornaments and tree toppers that show up every holiday season. Guess what I found? A lot of what appears to be empty Christmas frivolity actually abounds with deep religious significance and purpose.

Did you know that the legend of Santa Claus begins with a godly Christian man named Nicholas who was sainted by the Church? Did you know that the holly and poinsettias that fill our homes during the holidays spring from inspirational roots? With each new revelation, I found myself falling in love with Christmas all over again.

If you dream of a Christmas with less hustle and bustle, more heartfelt cheer, then join me on a 25-day journey as we rediscover the forgotten spiritual symbolism of this glorious holiday. Each day, you'll find a variety of craft ideas and personal applications for how to live these stories in your everyday life. Please invite your family, friends, and loved ones to join you on this quest for meaning and merriment! I hope this book brings you back to the heart of what Christmas is all about, and I hope it blesses your holiday season.

Preheat the oven, string up the lights, turn on your favorite Christmas tunes, and set out with me on a journey to create and fully appreciate the Christmas you've always dreamed of.

*Megan*

# CONTENTS

# CONTENTS

# CONTENTS

# CONTENTS

Silent Night, Holy

# CONTENTS

20
23
24

# { DAY } 1

# Advent Calendars

*To prepare our hearts for Christmas, we must cultivate a spirit of expectancy.*

—Reverend Handel H. Brown
*Keeping the Spirit of Christmas*

{DAY}

# 1

# WHAT IS THE PURPOSE OF ADVENT CALENDARS?

Okay. Full confession here. As I get older, I would say that it's almost more fun looking forward to Christmas than it is actually celebrating on Christmas Day. Don't get me wrong, I love Christmas morning and all the presents and joy like the rest of us. But the more I understand the historical significance and meaningful aspects of the holiday season, the more I enjoy the anticipation of Christmas. Does anyone else get goosebumps when you first spot Christmas decorations in the stores? I do! My kids and I love the first sight of our local Christmas tree lot beginning to go up or a Yule log cake in the grocery store bakery. It hints that something exciting is on the way.

Since around the fourth century, Christians have celebrated Advent as a time of anticipation and preparation. German Protestants in the mid-nineteenth century were likely the first to use Advent calendars, after using all sorts of creative ways to mark these important days of the Christian year. Parents can use Advent calendars as a teachable tool that gives their kids something to look forward to each day while also reflecting on the big day approaching and all it symbolizes.

We see Advent calendars in many shapes and sizes during the Christmas season. Each day from November 30 to December 25 has a little door to open. Behind each door is a chocolate candy, part of a picture, a tiny toy—some Advent calendars even offer a selection of teas. But rather than being about treats or trinkets, the calendar is a kind of devotional. The word *advent*, which comes from Latin, means "coming to" or "arriving at." Advent, then, is a time of anticipation when we look forward to the arrival of Jesus.

{ DAY }
1

# Create a Family Advent Calendar

*This year, consider turning your Advent calendar into a gratitude calendar. As you open the door for each day, think of one thing to be grateful for as you look forward to Christmas Day. Another fun addition to the typical Advent calendar is to create your own with Christmas activities. Plan ahead by asking family members in November what their favorite Christmas traditions are, then assign one of those activities to each day of Advent. For example, December 1 might be ice skating; December 2 might be watching a Christmas movie. Another idea perfect for young children is to create a paper chain for each day of Advent. Using red and green paper, make twenty-five paper loops and tear one off each day as you count down to Christmas.*

# {DAY} 2

# CANDY CANE

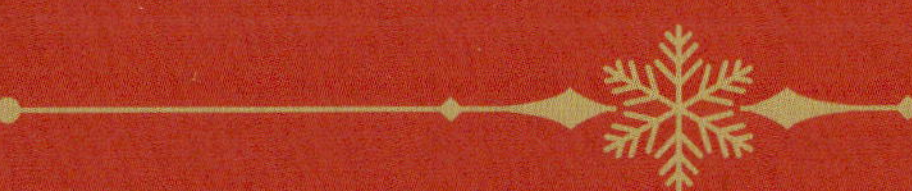

*Look at the candy cane, what do you see?*
*Stripes that are red, like the blood shed for me.*
*White for my Savior, who is sinless and pure.*
*"J" is for Jesus My Lord, that's for sure!*
*Turn it around and a staff you will see.*
*Jesus my shepherd who was born for me.*

—Author unknown

{ DAY }
2

# WHAT CLUES ARE IN THE CANDY CANE?

We've all heard of an Easter egg hunt, but a candy cane hunt has become one of my favorite holiday traditions. We sprinkle candy canes all over our back lawn, and at dusk we invite the neighborhood kids to come over with flashlights to try to find as many candy canes as they can. We give a prize to the child who finds the most. Afterward, when the kids have settled down and are enjoying their treats, we talk about what religious significance we can find in the candy.

According to one legend, around 1670 a choirmaster at the Cologne Cathedral in Germany bent one end of a peppermint candy stick into a curve to represent a shepherd's hook. And then when he turned the candy "hook" upside down, he explained that it became a J for Jesus. It is said that the choirmaster used the candy to hold the children's attention as they learned about the birth of Jesus.

During the nineteenth century, Christmas cards featured all-white candy canes. We can find meaning in the colors of today's typical candy canes: the white symbolizes the purity of Jesus, while the red represents the blood Jesus shed on the cross. Sometimes, a green stripe is added, which can signify that Jesus is an everlasting gift from God. The candy cane is much more than just a peppermint treat—it reminds us of the gift of Jesus.

{ DAY }
2

# Create Memories with a Candy Cane Hunt

*Add a dash of adventure to your holiday celebration this year. Imagine the excitement as friends and family race to uncover hidden treats, laughing and searching high and low for those sweet holiday treasures. I started by inviting families we knew from our neighborhood, but you could also make it a school or church activity. Even hiding candy canes around the house can be a fun challenge for your family. Once the hunt is over, use the moment to invite others to share why Jesus and the Christmas season are important to them.*

{ DAY }

# 3

# GINGERBREAD

*One day, the cook went into the kitchen to make some gingerbread.*

—Robert Gaston Herbert
*The Gingerbread Man*

## { DAY } 3

# WHY DO WE LOVE GINGERBREAD?

Building and decorating a gingerbread house with cookies, icing, and candy is a rewarding, creative experience. I have such fun decorating gingerbread houses with my three kiddos each year! We usually keep it pretty basic, as my young kids tend to start eating all the decorations if we try to add too much complexity. But it's a fun and simple way to build something together during the holidays.

Gingerbread is a perfect reminder of the warmth and joy that Christmas brings. Just the scent of gingerbread coming out of the oven is enough to make you feel as if you are being hugged by your home. One legend tells us that during the fifteenth century, unmarried girls would use gingerbread to find their future spouse. They would bake man-shaped cookies that were displayed at street fairs, with the superstition that the man who ate the cookie would fall in love with the woman who had baked it. During the seventeenth century, gingerbread was shaped into the image of religious icons, and the act of baking it was considered a sacred practice. Restrictions concerning the baking of gingerbread were enforced by the authorities. Only guild bakers were permitted to bake gingerbread during the calendar year. The edict was waived during Christmas and Easter, when everyone was allowed to bake the tasty, aromatic concoction.

Whether you're married or single this Christmas season, whether you're trying to keep little hands out of the frosting or crafting elaborate gingerbread castles, each time you catch the scent of gingerbread, remember the warmth that fills our kitchens and hearts during this special time of year.

{ DAY }
3

# Recruit Your Taste Testers

*Gingerbread cookies fill the home with the sweetest scent. Here's a favorite gingerbread cookie recipe straight from my house to yours!*

*And for the single folks—who's up for trying the gingerbread "find-your-future-spouse" taste test? If you are, let me know how it turns out!*

{DAY}
3

# GINGERBREAD COOKIE RECIPE

from the kitchen of Megan's Auntie Sherry

*INGREDIENTS*

1 cup shortening

1 cup molasses

1 tsp. baking soda

½ cup hot water

1 cup sugar

1 egg

1 tsp. vanilla

1 tsp. cinnamon

½ tsp. ginger

¼ tsp. cloves

1 tsp. salt

5½ cups flour

*DIRECTIONS*

Bring shortening and molasses to boil in a large pan. Boil for 1 minute. Remove from heat.

In a small bowl, mix baking soda into the water. Add to the molasses mixture. (Careful, this will bubble up quite a bit!)

Mix in remaining ingredients, all but the flour.

Mix in flour. The dough stiffens as it hardens.

Roll the dough to about ¼ inch thick. Using a cookie cutter, cut gingerbread men shapes from the dough. Place them on lightly greased cookie sheets.

Bake at 375° for 8–10 min.

Decorate with icing and candies after the cookies have cooled.

# { DAY } 4

# *Evergreens*

*O Christmas tree,*
*O Christmas tree,*
*how lovely*
*are your branches!*

—Lyrics by Ernst Anschütz

{ DAY }

# 4

# WHY DO WE DECORATE CHRISTMAS TREES?

When we were in our twenties, my husband Brian and I lived in a one-bedroom apartment in New York City. The apartment was so tiny, we really did not think a full Christmas tree would fit, but I was determined to have one. One day, I found the skinniest fake Christmas tree I have ever seen, as skinny as a single coat rack. But by golly I bought it and placed it in the corner of our apartment and decorated it up!

We always decorate our Christmas trees with lights and colors to create a beautiful centerpiece in our home. But when and why did people start decorating evergreens? One popular legend has it that in the sixteenth century, Martin Luther was walking to his home in Wittenberg, Germany, when he noticed how beautiful the evergreen trees looked with starlight and moonlight sparkling on branches dusted with snow. Luther decided to recreate this vision. He chopped down a tree, took it inside, attached candles to the branches, and then lit the candles. How much of the legend is apocryphal doesn't really matter because what the world got out of it is the beautiful tradition of decorating trees for Christmas.

Americans caught on to the idea when an illustration of Prince Albert's tree showed up in the newspapers. Prince Albert, who was German, brought this tradition to England when he married Queen Victoria. Eventually, Americans began to decorate their homes in the same way.

Christmas is the holiday that celebrates the birth of Christ, who is the Savior of the world. A tree represents life. The evergreen, with its always-green needles, reminds us of the everlasting love of God, even in the dead of whatever "winter" of our lives we might be going through, and of the hopeful fact that spring is on the way. Many people associate the triangular shape of a lighted evergreen with the Trinity: Father, Son, and Holy Spirit. At a basic level, a tree of lights signals hope during the dark months of winter.

As you trim your tree, enjoy the woody pine fragrance, bask in the glow of the lights tucked all throughout its limbs, and say thank you for the gift of life that is symbolized right there in your home.

{DAY}
4
Bless my family

# Trim Your Tree with Faith

*This year, brainstorm with your family how you can customize your Christmas tree to reflect your faith. Perhaps seek out religious-themed ornaments—a tree decorated in angels and stars of all shapes and sizes would look lovely. Or you might decide to tuck the laminated holy cards of all your favorite saints among the boughs of your tree. Everyone in the family could write and illustrate their favorite prayer, and then make the prayers into ornaments. A good way to focus children on this project is to find the special prayer of the saint whose feast day is the same as the child's birthdate.*

# { DAY } 5 CANDLES

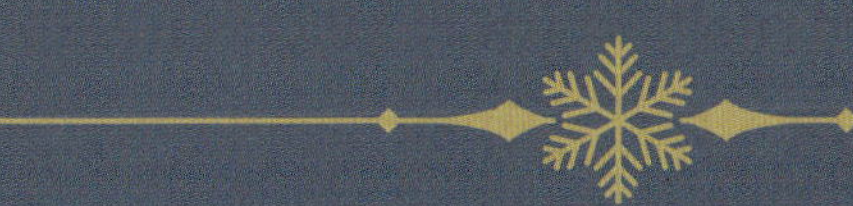

*You are the light of the world.*

—Matthew 5:14

{ DAY }
5

# WHAT IS THE MEANING OF CANDLES AT CHRISTMAS?

There is nothing quite as beautiful, peaceful, or spiritual as a candlelight service on Christmas Eve. I have special memories of attending midnight Mass with my family. The lights would dim, and the entire congregation would hold candles while singing "Silent Night." It was a truly sacred moment. Nowadays, with little ones who can't stay up until midnight, we find an earlier candlelight service at a local church. I sometimes grow nostalgic for those late-night services, but coming together as a family to worship and praise the birth of Jesus on Christmas Eve is a beautiful experience, no matter the time. Plus, it gives me a chance to light a candle or two in my own window at home.

During colonial times in America, placing candles in windows often signaled to travelers that the home was a welcoming place where they could find a meal and a place to rest. In Ireland during the seventeenth and eighteenth centuries, when Catholicism was suppressed under British rule, families would place a candle in the window as a discreet signal to priests that their home was a safe place to celebrate Mass. If questioned by British authorities, the families would explain that the candle was a symbol of welcoming the Holy Family (Jesus, Mary, and Joseph) into their home. Many Irish immigrants to America brought this tradition with them and it became symbolic of hospitality to all during the Christmas season.

Christmas brings us the gift of light, a reminder that the glow of a single candle conquers even the blackest darkness. Coming as it does after the winter solstice, Christmas, which is nothing less than the birth of the Light of the World, stands in stark contrast to the darkest time of the calendar year. Just as the newborn Jesus signifies the open arms of love and inclusiveness, so too can we spread the light of love and welcome with the flickering light of a candle in the window.

{ DAY }
5

# Let Your Love Shine

*The holidays can be difficult if a dear friend, family member, or pet has passed away. But there are many beautiful ways to keep their memory alive. Place a candle in the window of your home to honor the memory of the one who has passed. (Use a flameless candle for safety.) Make this a holiday tradition with your children. We do this with a photo of my grandparents, who have all passed away. A special place of honor with a candle goes to my Grandpa Don, who served as a Marine in World War II. Consider placing a framed photo of this special someone next to your candle. Suddenly something that seemed sad can turn into a sweet Christmas tradition. Or, what about trying to "be a light" in your community? Volunteer with the local food bank or another charity. The point is to find ways to shine your light, even if only for the sake of your family, by doing something unexpected and thoughtful.*

nta,
e been
good.

{ DAY }

# 6

# Santa Claus

*Everybody loves St. Nicholas, because St. Nicholas loves everybody.*

—Father Andrew Phillips
*Archpriest of St. John's Orthodox Church in Colchester, Essex, England*

{ DAY }

# 6

## WAS THERE A REAL SANTA CLAUS?

The jolly, red-suited Santa Claus is based on a compassionate man whom we know today as St. Nicholas, and who lived more than a thousand years ago. Nicholas was likely born sometime around AD 270 in Patara, near Myra in modern-day Turkey. One version of the St. Nicholas legend says that he was born into a wealthy family but gave away all his inherited wealth and then traveled the countryside helping the poor and sick. Another version has Nicholas visiting the home of a poor man late at night, when he and his three daughters were all asleep. Nicholas is said to have anonymously dropped gold coins into their shoes, money that would be used as the young ladies' dowry. Because of his strong faith, wisdom, generosity, and servant leadership, St. Nicholas is admired and honored throughout the world. In the Catholic Church, December 6—the day of his death in 343—is the feast day of St. Nicholas. Celebrations take on various manifestations depending on the country, but often there is an exchange of gifts, a tradition meant to pay tribute to the Christian bishop known for gift-giving. As you notice depictions of St. Nicholas popping up all over town, consider how you and your family can be generous to people in your own community.

{ DAY }
6

# Get to Know Santa

*Share the story of St. Nicholas's life by locating on a globe or atlas all the countries where St. Nicholas traditions are celebrated, and discuss how St. Nicholas is honored on his feast day in those cultures.*

*In Poland, children awaken on St. Nicholas Day to find a gift under their pillow. You and your kids can enact this custom. After they have fallen asleep, sneak a small surprise underneath their pillow.*

*In the Netherlands and Belgium, children leave a hat and carrots next to their shoes beside the door, with the carrot intended for St. Nicholas's horse. While your kids sleep, leave a note and small treats outside their bedroom.*

*In the United States and many other countries, children leave shoes by the door the night before St. Nicholas Day. Have your kids place their shoes by the front door or outside their bedroom and fill them with a few surprises as they sleep.*

{ DAY }

# CARDINALS

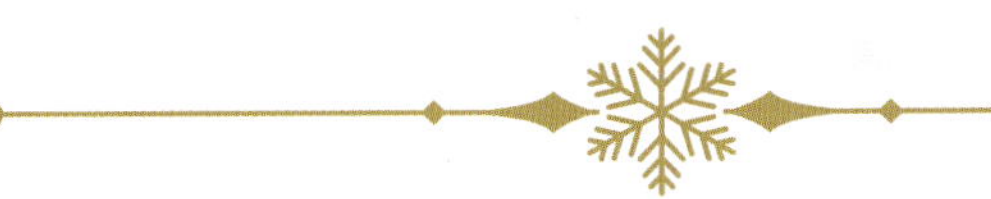

*Cardinals appear when angels are near.*

–Victoria McGovern

{ DAY }
7

# WHY IS THE CARDINAL ASSOCIATED WITH CHRISTMAS?

My four-year-old daughter loves catching sight of cardinals outside. The beautiful bold red color of a cardinal's feathers against the background of a green tree makes the bird easy to spot. It's not surprising, then, that the cardinal is a familiar character in Christmas decorations. The bird even got its name because its striking color reminded early European settlers of the vestments, red mittens, and caps worn by Roman Catholic bishops. The fact that cardinals are typically faithful to and fiercely protective of their mates, especially while they are nesting and caring for their hatchlings, also reminds us of Christ's fidelity to God the Father as well as his eternal love for us all.

Many people believe that seeing a cardinal nearby is a sign from a loved one who has passed on. People will often place cardinal decorations in their Christmas trees, wreaths, and garlands as a remembrance of loved ones who have passed.

Let these beautiful birds prompt you to reflect upon the many ways God has been faithful to you. Take a moment now, and every time you catch sight of a red cardinal and his mate, to remember God's faithfulness to you and to those you love.

{ DAY }

# 7

# Cardinal Memories

*Celebrate the season by creating a heartfelt tribute to family and friends with a special spot on your Christmas tree. Decorate your tree with a few cardinal ornaments to symbolize loved ones watching over your family. Gather a piece of festive paper, and with your children, make a list of family members, friends, or pets you want to honor this season. Encourage each child to share a memory or message as you write the names together. Once finished, tuck the remembrance—perhaps rolled into a small scroll and tied with a ribbon—on the boughs beside the cardinal ornaments, keeping those who have touched your lives close during the holidays.*

# { DAY }

# 8

# *Angels*

*And [the angel]*
*came to her and said,*
*"Greetings, favored one!*
*The Lord is with you."*

–Luke 1:28

{ DAY }
8

# WHY DO WE USE ANGEL DECORATIONS?

When I was about twelve years old, my church put on a "walk-thru Bethlehem" live nativity scene, with different scenes of the story of Jesus's birth set up outside the church. I remember it vividly. Yours truly was given the role of the angel Gabriel! On opening night, I decided I was going to do a twirl dance as I entered, which would make my white sheet costume billow and float behind me. Was this biblically accurate? No. Did I run it past the church first? No again. So there I was, twirling and whirling as I delivered those famous lines to Mary: "Greetings, favored one! The Lord is with you."

After one of our performances, I overheard a child ask their father about my scene. I remember distinctly his answer: "This is the moment Mary realizes she has been chosen—but she is not alone. This angel is the first to offer her protection and strength." I had not thought of it this way before. Gabriel was "seeing" Mary that night when he appeared to her. He was doing what angels do: reminding us that we are not alone, that we are seen and loved.

Maybe this is why to me one of the most comforting symbols of the Christmas season is the presence of angels. Angels announced and heralded Jesus's forthcoming birth. The angel Gabriel also appeared to Zechariah and informed him that his wife, Elizabeth, would give birth to John the Baptist, who would prepare the people for Jesus's coming. An angel also appeared to the shepherds on the hillsides outside Bethlehem on the night Jesus was born, which inspired many Christmas carols, including "Hark! The Herald Angels Sing" and "Angels We Have Heard on High." The angel serves as a messenger of good news from heaven during the Christmas story.

In the classic Christmas movie *It's A Wonderful Life*, Clarence, the personal angel of the main character, George Bailey, takes George on a time-travel journey through his life. Clarence helps George see what the world would have been like without him in it, and George realizes the positive impact his life has had on the people who live in his hometown. Angels present during the holiday season remind us of the unseen heavenly realm that is always hovering protectively and looking out for us.

{DAY}
8

# Invite the Angels In

*This year, as you decorate your Christmas tree, take a moment to celebrate the role of angels in the Christmas story. When it's time to place the angel at the top, recount the appearance of angels in the nativity story and the messages of God's love and guidance they herald. Afterward, pop some popcorn, gather together, and watch* It's A Wonderful Life. *Allow the story to spotlight the powerful influence of angelic presence and inspire a greater awareness of gratitude.*

# { DAY } 9

# *Poinsettia*

*And every Christmas to
this day, the red stars shine on
top of green branches in Mexico.
The people call the plants*
la Flor de Nochebuena–
*the Flower of the Holy Night–
the poinsettia.*

–Tomie dePaola
*The Legend of the Poinsettia*

{ DAY }

9

# WHAT'S THE STORY BEHIND THE POINSETTIA?

The legend of the poinsettia tells the story of a Mexican girl named Pepita who was sad because she had no present to give the baby Jesus at the Christmas Eve services. As she made her way to the chapel, Pepita's cousin Pedro tried to cheer her up. "Pepita," he said, "I'm sure that even the smallest gift, given by someone who loves him, will make Jesus happy."

Pedro's wise counsel lifted Pepita's spirits. Inspired by hope, she picked a handful of roadside weeds and gathered them into a small bouquet. Though she felt small and unworthy as she approached the altar, Pepita held on to the words Pedro had said for courage. She knelt before the *nacimiento*—the nativity scene—bowed her head, and placed the bouquet on the floor.

Suddenly, the weeds flowered with brilliant red petals, so big it seemed as if they were reaching for the Holy Family. Stunned by the sight, everyone in the chapel was convinced that they had seen a miracle. From that day on, the humble weeds that burst into glorious crimson flowers became known as the *Flores de la Nochebuena*, or the Flowers of the Holy Night.

The growth cycle of the poinsettia, with its dormant phase followed by a seemingly impossible reflowering, metaphorically reflects the Death and Resurrection of Christ. Potted plants that are shut away in a darkened environment in October will reward their patient caretakers with brilliant blossoms at Christmastime.

Christmas miracles come in all shapes and sizes, and they always bring the gift of wonder. May we slow down long enough to allow wonder enter into our days, and give proper notice to the special moments that clamor for our attention.

{ DAY }
9

# Adorn Your Home with Poinsettias

*Poinsettias typically achieve their first blooms in October, which the faithful look upon as a herald of the coming Christmas season. The shape of the poinsettia flower is said to resemble the Star of Bethlehem, and its scarlet leaves symbolize the blood of Jesus. In the Mexican tradition, poinsettias are known as the Christmas Eve flower.*

*In addition to decorating your home with these beautiful plants, a fun craft can be drawing poinsettias on paper. Find an easy template online, get out the red crayons, and while you draw, share with your family the story of Pepita.*

# { DAY } 10

# MISTLETOE

*Love is patient; love is kind;*
*love is not envious or boastful or*
*arrogant or rude. It does not insist*
*on its own way; it is not irritable or resentful;*
*it does not rejoice in wrongdoing,*
*but rejoices in the truth. It bears all things,*
*believes all things, hopes all things,*
*endures all things. Love never ends.*

—1 Corinthians 13:4–8

{ DAY }

# 10

# IS MISTLETOE JUST FOR KISSING?

Mistletoe is a fascinating plant. It's an aerial parasite, with no roots of its own, that can bloom in all kinds of weather. It lives off the tree to which it attaches itself, and without that tree, it would die. This fact of nature makes it easy to understand why we see mistletoe as a Christmas symbol of our love, which exists only because God loves us. God, who is love, created us in love and caused us to be able to love.

The early Greeks, as well as the Celtic Druids, used the plant to enhance fertility, which may have something to do with the custom of couples kissing underneath the plant. While we associate mistletoe today with an infatuated type of love, we can remember the words of Corinthians and think also of peace, faith, hope, and life.

{ DAY }
10

# Spread Love and Hope with Mistletoe Moments

*Hanging mistletoe around your home is a fun way to bring holiday cheer, but this year, let it serve as more than a kissing corner. Known for thriving even in the coldest months, the message of mistletoe is to take heart and spread hope. Each time you or a loved one passes beneath a sprig of mistletoe, take a moment to reflect on how you can spread kindness and brotherly love. Whether it's lending a hand to a neighbor, sharing a meal with someone in need, or offering a smile, let your mistletoe moments remind you to "pay it forward" and brighten someone's day.*

# { DAY } 11

# *Snowflakes*

*Now you are the body of Christ and individually members of it.*

–1 Corinthians 12:27

## { DAY } 11

# HOW DO WE KNOW ALL SNOWFLAKES ARE UNIQUE?

If you live in an area that typically sees snow, there is nothing quite so magical as the first snowfall of the holiday season. When we take a closer look at snow, we see individual snowflakes that make a big impact on the world when they stick together.

The first known photographer of snowflakes was a man named Wilson Bentley. He lived on a farm in Vermont where snowfall was plentiful, and he loved to observe snowflakes. His parents spent their savings on a camera so that Bentley could photograph his beloved snow. Explaining the purpose behind his fascination and research, Bentley said, "Under the microscope, I found that snowflakes were miracles of beauty, and it seemed a shame that this beauty should not be seen and appreciated by others." His work helped us learn that every snowflake is a unique shape or pattern.

In Christianity, each believer is seen as an essential part of the Body of Christ, and we are meant to work together to accomplish God's work in the world. We teach children that each person is made in God's image, and that God created them to be unique individuals—sort of like how no two snowflakes are alike. God's ability to create is infinite, and we can praise and thank God for the limitless diversity in the universe.

{ DAY }
11

# Study a Snowflake

*If snow graces your area this holiday season, grab a magnifying glass, go outside while the snow is falling, and marvel at the unique, intricate beauty of each snowflake. For those in warmer climates, reading the Caldecott Medal–winning* Snowflake Bentley *by Jacqueline Briggs Martin together can capture the same magic. As you explore the wonders of snowflakes, talk about how these delicate creations serve as reminders of our own uniqueness and beauty. Just like snowflakes, each of us is a one-of-a-kind gift from God, reflecting life's extraordinary design.*

# {DAY} 12 BELLS

*I heard the bells on Christmas Day*
*Their old, familiar carols play,*
*And wild and sweet*
*The words repeat*
*Of peace on earth, good-will to men!*

—Henry Wadsworth Longfellow
"Christmas Bells"

{DAY}
12

# WHY DID BELLS BECOME IMPORTANT AT CHRISTMAS?

My children named their one and only cat Jingle. Jingle wore a collar with a little silver bell on it, a conscious decision we made so that we always knew when she was around. But we came to love the tinkling of her collar bell as the sweetest sound in all the house.

There is something so magical about hearing bells ringing at Christmastime. The sounds of church bells, sleigh bells, and handbells fill the air. It's long been a tradition to ring bells at midnight on Christmas Eve to celebrate the birth of Jesus. Their beautiful, clear sound can symbolize what the angels may have sounded like when they proclaimed, "Glory to God in the highest heaven, and on earth peace among those whom he favors!" (Luke 2:14).

But Henry Wadsworth Longfellow's poem reminds us that even the most celebratory of bells can ring out with messages that are also solemn, sacred, and soulful. Longfellow wrote this famous poem when he was both mourning the death of his wife and keeping watch over his son, whose life hung in the balance after being seriously injured during the American Civil War. Sitting at his hospitalized son's bedside, Longfellow was praying for his son's recovery when he "heard the bells on Christmas Day." The sound of those bells rang forth a reminder of nothing less than hope—hope that was his even at this moment of desperation, and all because of the baby born so long ago in Bethlehem.

{ DAY }

# 12

# Embrace the Jingle Jangle

*Loop ribbons of jingle bells around door handles. Change your phone alarms and alerts to the sound of bells ringing. Tie a sweet little jingle bell to your purse handle or key ring. Then, every time you hear a bell ringing, allow those chimes to reach inside your heart and bring you a moment of joy, happiness, and hope. Let the bells remind you that God is watching over you, your loved ones, and all of us—at Christmastime, and always.*

{ DAY }

# 13

# Gifts of Fruit

*Love is a fruit in season*
*at all times,*
*and within reach*
*of every hand.*

—Mother Teresa

{ DAY }
13

## WHY IS FRUIT GIFTED DURING THE HOLIDAYS?

My family on my mother's side hails from Denmark. They were potato farmers, and when the harvest was scarce, the children received only an orange in their stocking at Christmas. Even so, the orange brought much pleasure. Fruit was considered a luxury of abundance, and when it was gifted, it served as a reminder to enjoy the simple pleasures in life. Sometimes fruit was chosen as a very special gift because it was intended as a gesture of wishes for good luck and prosperity.

Fruit reminds us of the nine fruits of the spirit: love, joy, peace, patience, kindness, goodness, faithfulness, gentleness, and self-control. People often give fruit baskets and fruitcake as gifts at Christmas, as they remind us of God's abundance and blessings, and that the harvest was good, and now we can enjoy the fruits of the farmers' labors.

Bags of clementines are often front and center in grocery stores during the holidays. Did you know these hark back to the days of Saint Nicholas? The orange fruit reminds us of the gold coins Nicholas concealed in bags and left for the three daughters of a devoted father who couldn't pay their dowries.

{ DAY }
13

# Honor the "Orange-ins" of Christmas

*Give a respectful nod to the origins of*
*a Christmas that was considered fruitful*
*no matter how humble by featuring*
*fruit dishes in your holiday meals,*
*adorning your table and kitchen counter*
*with bowls of fresh fruit,*
*and sending fruit baskets as gifts.*

# { DAY } 14

# Bread

*The best of all gifts around*
*any Christmas tree:*
*the presence of a happy family*
*all wrapped up in each other.*

—William E. Vaughan, aka Burton Hillis

{DAY}
14

## WHERE DID ALL THE FANCY BREAD COME FROM?

My husband's French-Canadian family has a long-standing tradition of making cinnamon rolls at Christmastime. Our Aunt Marg prepares them over several days and makes it a family activity, teaching grandkids and cousins just the right way to prepare the dough. Then, on Christmas Eve, the family attends midnight Mass and comes home to freshly baked, warm cinnamon rolls.

Christmas pastries made with flour call to mind the many uses of bread in Scripture. The Jewish people offered up to God cakes made with flour and oil. The Israelites took their unleavened loaves with them when they fled Egypt, an event that is commemorated each year in the Feast of Unleavened Bread. The manna in the desert tasted like wafers made with honey. Elijah performed a miracle in which a widow's flour did not run out during a time of famine. Jesus multiplied loaves twice in Scripture, and repeatedly explained that he is the Bread of Life, which we celebrate during the Eucharist.

This rich history of the significance of flour is present with every bite of Christmas pastries, and we are reminded that God provides our daily bread.

{ DAY }
14

# Fire Up Your Oven!

*If you don't already have a designated holiday baking event with your family, consider this your nudge to schedule one! Some families start their Christmas baking on Thanksgiving weekend. Maybe you'd like to set the first Sunday of each month in the fall as your "Family Bake Time." Sharing favorite recipes, trying new ones with the encouragement of a cheering squad, and handing down generations-old baking tips are tangible expressions of love and connection. And every time we break bread (or cookies!) together, in essence, we are following the example of the adult Jesus, who wouldn't dream of letting anyone go home hungry, and who gives himself to us every time we break bread together in the form of the Eucharist.*

*As for me and my family, one recipe we will be making is my Aunt Marg's delicious cinnamon rolls, and you are cordially invited to join us in sticky deliciousness.*

{DAY}
14

# AUNT MARG'S CINNAMON ROLLS

*INGREDIENTS*

3 packages of yeast

¾ cup very warm water + ¾ tsp. sugar

2 cups scalded milk

1¾ cups warm water

5 Tbs. sugar

1 Tbs. + 2 tsp. salt

4 to 5 Tbs. margarine or butter

Approximately 11 to 13 cups bread flour

*DIRECTIONS*

Put the yeast in a small bowl and add the very warm water and ¾ tsp. sugar. Mix well until the yeast is dissolved. Set aside to raise.

Scald the 2 cups of milk.

Put the sugar, salt, and margarine in a large mixing bowl. Add the scalded milk. Stir until the margarine is melted and the salt and sugar are dissolved. Add the 1¾ cups warm water and stir.

Now add a couple cups of flour and stir, then stir in the raised yeast mixture. Continue adding flour. When it becomes too difficult to stir, place the dough onto a well-floured surface. Continue adding flour, mixing with your hands, until the dough is no longer sticky and moist.

Knead the dough with your hands for about 8 minutes or until the dough feels soft and smooth. Place the dough in a large, well-greased bowl with a cover. The bowl should be large enough to allow for the dough to rise to at least double in size. Set the bowl in a warm place. It will take about 2 hours for the dough to rise.

When the dough is raised, knead the dough down by taking the outer edges of the dough and "folding" it in and over on top; this will take the air out of the dough. Now flip the dough over, place it back in the bowl, cover the bowl, and let it rise again for about 2 hours.

It is now time to build your rolls. You will need butter or margarine, brown sugar (preferably dark brown), and cinnamon. Once again, flour your working surface. Using a slicing knife and a rolling pin, cut off a piece of dough large enough to roll out into an elongated shape and flat enough to roll up into a jelly roll style. Butter the dough, cover it with brown sugar, and sprinkle on some cinnamon. Starting from the bottom of your flattened-out dough, roll it up into a tube and cut slices off to make the rolls. Place them onto a well-greased 9 x 13 (or larger) pan. Continue this process until the pan is filled. Do not crowd them; leave room for the rolls to rise.

This recipe should fill 2 pans.

Preheat the oven to 350 degrees. The rolls will once again rise, filling in the spaces on the pans. When the oven is ready, place the pans on the middle rack and bake for about 35 minutes or until the rolls are browned on top.

Remove the rolls from the oven and turn them upside down on racks to cool. I like to put them on cotton dish towels to keep them fresher after they have cooled. After the rolls have cooled a bit, I also put wax paper over the top to keep the caramel from getting all over the towels. Once they are completely cooled, wrap them in the dish towels and put them in a plastic bag to help them stay fresh.

My husband, Brian, makes Aunt Marg's Cinnamon Rolls every holiday season in the same way as he was taught by his Aunt Marg.

Enjoy with your family!

{ DAY }

# 15

# 12 DAYS *of Christmas*

*On the first day of Christmas
my true love sent to me
a partridge in a pear tree.*

—Anonymous

# WHY EXACTLY ARE THERE 12 DAYS OF CHRISTMAS?

At first listen, "The 12 Days of Christmas" may seem like just a silly song, but the song is referring to the time between the birth of Jesus on December 25 and the coming of the Magi on January 6, otherwise known as the Epiphany. We often think of the Christmas season as extending from Advent to Christmas Day, but appreciating the 12 days between Christmas and Epiphany allows us time to extend the joy beyond December 25. In some cultures, the Christmas season very definitely extends throughout these 12 days, and Epiphany is celebrated with community-wide festivities including joyous parades and church ceremonies.

The origin of the 12-day period may trace back to the fourth century when Christians held both Christmas and the Epiphany in high regard, though Christians at the time couldn't agree on what those dates were. In 567, during the Council of Tours, Christian leaders formalized the 12-day festal period beginning on December 25 and ending on Twelfth Night, during the evening of January 5. This period of time was deemed sacred and was intended to emphasize the ongoing celebration of Jesus's birth and, at the same time, help counter-balance some of the secular and pagan festivals that occurred around this time.

Over the years, "The 12 Days of Christmas" has become a staple of the holiday season. The origins of the song are clouded in mystery; many believe it started as an eighteenth-century folk song. Some people, especially in modern times, have assigned a religious connotation to the various days. One of the most popular interpretations comes from a Canadian teacher who, in 1979, wrote an article on how to decode the song. Though scholars reject the idea that there is any hidden code in the verses of the well-known carol (grinches), I still like the ideas he set forth and present them here as a way of keeping Jesus and the season in the song. What follows is a quick breakdown of the symbols and their interpretative meanings.

## PARTRIDGE IN A PEAR TREE

represents Jesus, the Son of God. Christ is presented as a mother partridge, a bird that will die to protect its young.

## TWO TURTLEDOVES

represent the Old and New Testaments.

## THREE FRENCH HENS

represent faith, hope, and love (1 Corinthians 13:13).

## FOUR CALLING BIRDS

are Matthew, Mark, Luke, and John.

## FIVE GOLDEN RINGS

stand for the Pentateuch, the first five books of the Old Testament.

## SIX GEESE A-LAYING

is code for the six days of creation.

## SEVEN SWANS A-SWIMMING

signals the gifts of the Holy Spirit: prophecy, ministry, teaching, exhortation, giving, leading, and compassion. Serene and graceful, swans are a fitting analogy to the Holy Spirit.

## EIGHT MAIDS A-MILKING

stand for the eight Beatitudes taught by Jesus at the Sermon on the Mount.

## NINE LADIES DANCING

are the nine gifts of the Holy Spirit: love, joy, peace, patience, kindness, goodness, faithfulness, gentleness, and self-control.

## TEN LORDS A-LEAPING

represent the Ten Commandments.

## ELEVEN PIPERS PIPING

stand for the eleven apostles who were left after Judas betrayed Jesus.

## TWELVE DRUMMERS DRUMMING

refers to the twelve points of the Apostles' Creed.

{ DAY }
15

# Host a Festive "12 Days of Christmas" Celebration

*Bring the joy of the season to life with a "12 Days of Christmas" gathering for family and friends. Invite loved ones over for a cozy evening, complete with favorite holiday treats and a bit of holiday sparkle. Assign each guest one of the verses from the beloved carol and share the hidden meaning behind their verse. Encourage everyone to embrace their role by dressing up or bringing a prop that reflects their line in the song. When it's time to perform, each person will sing their verse with enthusiasm, adding a touch of personal flair. The evening culminates in a joyful group rendition of the song, with each participant explaining their verse's significance. It's a lively, interactive way to celebrate the spirit of Christmas, creating a memorable experience full of laughter, warmth, and holiday cheer!*

# { DAY } 16

# *Tinsel*

*Joy to the world,*
*The Lord is come!*
*Let earth receive her King!*

–Lyrics by Isaac Watts

{ DAY }

# 16

# WHAT'S THE BACKSTORY OF TINSEL?

There is no song quite so joyful as "Joy to the World"—rightly so! This beloved Christmas carol is a bold and boisterous celebration of the Good News. I reflect on all the times I have been sitting in church as the choir belts out this song. I don't think any song accurately reflects "belt out" better than this one, and you can't help but feel happy when you hear it. Tinsel brings me the same happiness.

The word *tinsel* comes from the French word *éntinceler*, which means "to sparkle," and tinsel was historically used on Christmas trees to magnify the flickering of candlelight.

Variations of a folktale existing in many cultures tell of a poor family with no money to decorate their Christmas tree. In the nighttime, spiders came and spun webs across the tree, and the silvery strands glistened in the morning light. These days, we can see in the glimmer of thin metallic strands of gold, silver, and red hanging from trees, bookshelves, garlands, and wreaths the echo of those humble decorations created by nature.

More importantly, the reflection of light given off by tinsel can remind us that the birth of Jesus is nothing less than the gleaming Hope of the World.

## {DAY} 16

# Take a Family "Joy Walk"

*Get your family bundled up and ready for a heartwarming "Joy Walk" through your neighborhood. As you stroll, take time to admire the festive lights and decorations, pointing out your favorites and sharing why they make you feel joyful. To add to the experience, bring along some hot cocoa or apple cider, and maybe wear your favorite Christmas sweater for an extra dose of cheer. Make it even more fun by turning tinsel into a festive scarf!*

*This simple tradition of reminding everyone to see the sparkle and share the joy could become a favorite part of your family's holiday season.*

{ DAY }

17

# Christmas Stockings

*The giver of every good and perfect gift has called upon us to mimic God's giving, by grace, through faith, and this is not of ourselves.*

–St. Nicholas of Myra

{ DAY }
17

# WHO STARTED THE TRADITION OF HANGING STOCKINGS?

To me, St. Nicholas possesses the testimony of grace like few others. The man on whom Santa Claus is based appears in earlier pages of this book, but I think you will agree that he deserves another day devoted to his story! I say this because it was Nicholas, a bishop of Myra, whose thoughtful generosity gave birth to the sweet tradition of Christmas stockings.

Every Christmas, many people imitate the legend of the stockings first filled by Nicholas of Myra by decorating fireplace mantles or other corners of their homes with stockings. Children all over the world rush to the fireplace on Christmas morning to take down their stockings and enjoy the treats and small presents stuffed inside. At first glance, this may seem like just another secular Christmas tradition connected to a commercialized Santa Claus. But this tradition reflects the story of the generous and merciful man who became St. Nicholas.

Legend has it that a poor man with three daughters lived in Nicholas's town, and the father could not afford to pay a dowry for his daughters to marry, which was an extreme disadvantage to the daughters in that society. One night, Nicholas secretly tossed gold coins into the stocking the daughters had hung over the fireplace to dry. The father discovered it was Nicholas who had gifted the coins and thereby saved his daughters, but Nicholas made him promise to keep his kind act a secret, as he did not want to bring attention to himself.

St. Nicholas performed many other acts of kindness during his lifetime. When you hang your Christmas stockings, say a prayer of thanks for the man whose gift of grace survives to this very day as a shining example of noticing our neighbors, and doing what we can to help them.

{DAY}
17

# Give Quietly Because the Quieter the Gift, the Happier the Heart

*This year, honor the spirit of St. Nicholas by turning Christmas into a season of quiet giving. Challenge your family to choose one or two people to surprise with Secret Santa gifts, delivered anonymously. These gifts don't need to be extravagant—homemade ornaments, cookies, or heartfelt notes can brighten someone's day. To deepen the experience, consider extending kindness to those who might not expect it. Is there someone in your life who could use a little Christmas cheer? Is there someone in your life to whom you can offer forgiveness? These are beautiful ways to spread the love that St. Nicholas embodied, and to bring a sense of grace and joy to your holiday season.*

CHEZ

# {DAY} 18

# A Christmas Carol

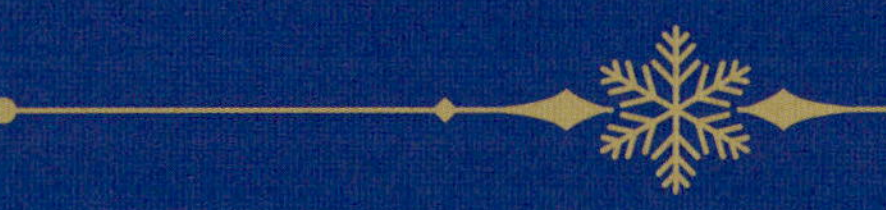

*I will honour Christmas in my heart, and try to keep it all year long. I will live in the Past, the Present and the Future. The Spirits of all Three shall strive within me.*

—Charles Dickens
*A Christmas Carol*

{ DAY }
18

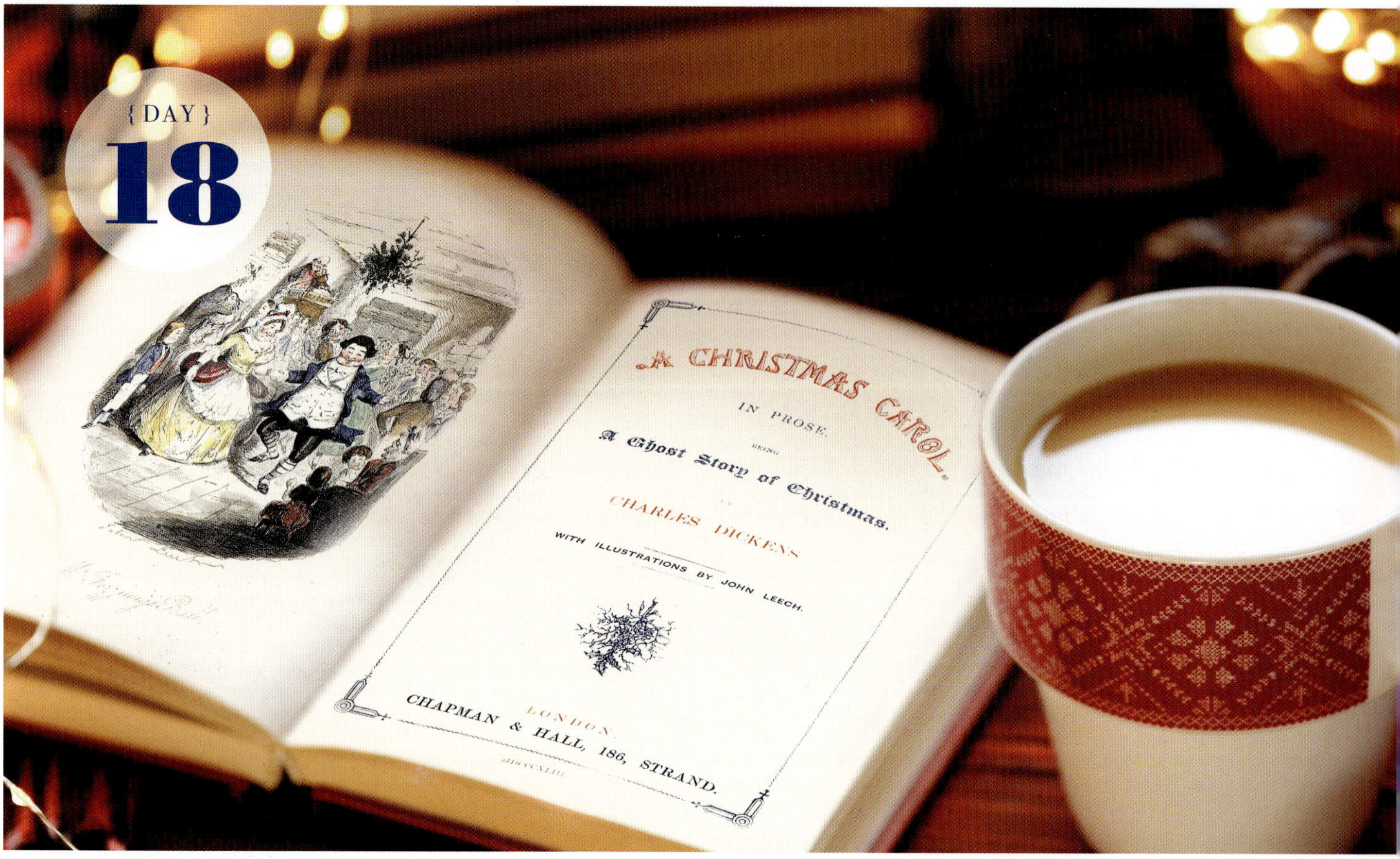
A CHRISTMAS CAROL
IN PROSE
A Ghost Story of Christmas.
CHARLES DICKENS
WITH ILLUSTRATIONS BY JOHN LEECH.
LONDON.
CHAPMAN & HALL, 186, STRAND.

OLD &
RARE
BOOKS

CITÉ
CARCASSONNE
Femmes

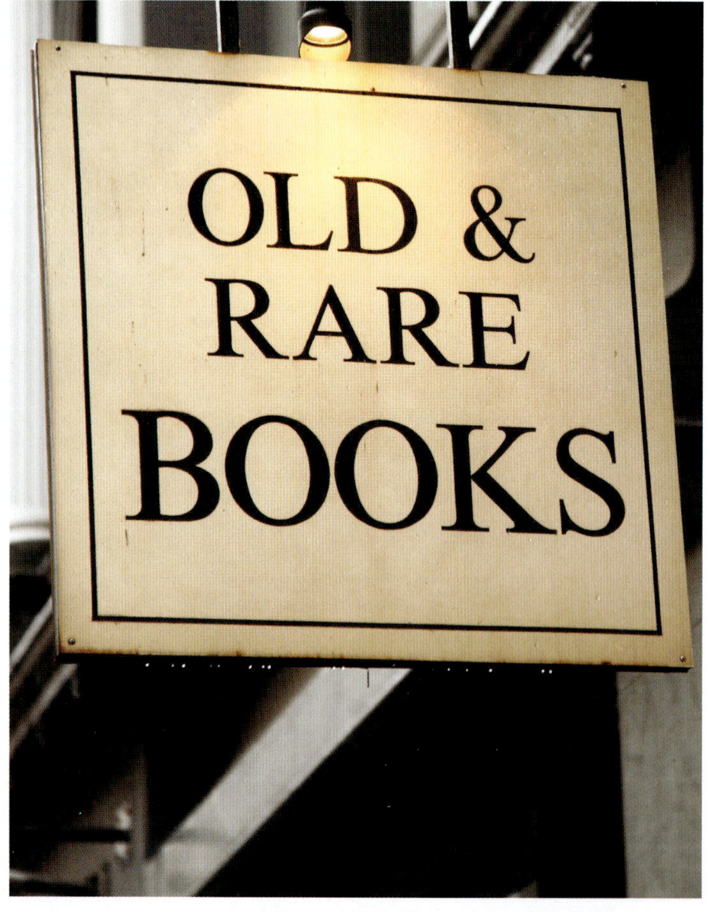

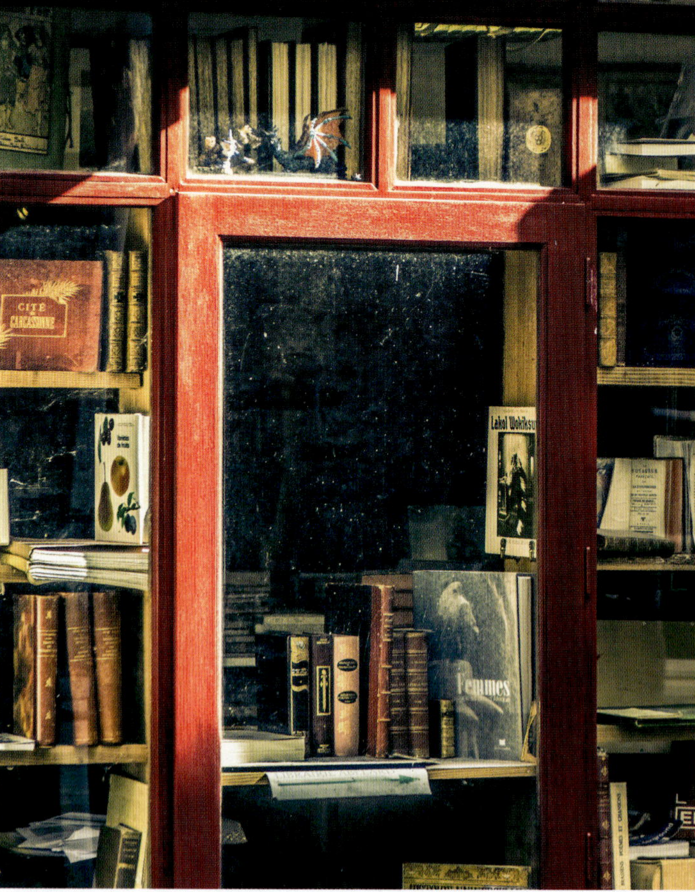

# WHY IS *A CHRISTMAS CAROL* SO POWERFUL?

I collect copies of Charles Dickens's book *A Christmas Carol*. Every time I travel to a city for my TV show *Small Town Christmas*, I love to find the local independent bookstore and scan the shelves for a copy of this iconic story. To me, there is no better representation of the gift of mercy than its main character, Ebenezer Scrooge.

At the beginning of the story, Scrooge is a heartless, lonely, embittered, and downright mean old man. He does not celebrate Christmas; indeed, he despises everything it stands for. Ebenezer's life takes a radical turn when he is awakened one night and taken on a journey by the Ghost of Christmas Past, the Ghost of Christmas Present, and the Ghost of Christmas Future. We are given glimpses of how childhood trauma slowly chipped away at his soul and stole his joy. How bitterness began to creep into his heart. How joylessness led to his isolation and misery. The Ghosts of Christmas help him see that unless he changes, he is doomed to die a lonely man. He awakens. It is Christmas morning, and Scrooge realizes he is being given a second chance at life. Scrooge is so thankful and happy that he begins to laugh uncontrollably, like a little kid. He then uses his position of privilege and wealth to spread Christmas joy and healing. Overnight, he becomes generous, kind, grateful, and vibrant—the polar opposite of the person he once was.

Have you ever experienced a really horrible nightmare, and then you wake up and realize it was just a dream? Relief washes over you. I imagine this was what Scrooge felt when he woke up. To me, this is the gift of Christmas—Jesus's birth. No matter how horrible we have been, Jesus's birth reminds us that we have been given the gift of a second chance. We can strive to live out everything the Christmas season offers, bless others with the spirit of gratitude and generosity, and fully dive into Christmas, as Ebenezer Scrooge did one life-changing Christmas morning.

{DAY}
18

# Make a Movie-with-a-Message Night

*Watch* A Christmas Carol *with your family. There are so many versions to choose from! My personal favorite is from 1951 starring Alastair Sim as Scrooge. A nice introduction to this story for your little children is to watch* The Muppet Christmas Carol. *For those who want a rousing musical version, try* Scrooge *starring Albert Finney. Star Trek "Trekkies" might enjoy Patrick Stewart as Scrooge in the 1999 version of* A Christmas Carol. *Finally, comedic actor Jim Carrey tried his hand at playing the old miser in the animated version that was released in 2009. (But beware! This one is really scary in some places.) In our household, though, the version that is on repeat throughout the holidays is the Disney version,* Mickey's Christmas Carol. *No matter what the version, this timeless tale never disappoints.*

# { DAY }
# 19

# The Nutcracker

*The nutcracker sits under*
*the holiday tree, a guardian*
*of childhood stories.*
*Feed him walnuts and he*
*will crack open a tale.*

—Vera Nazarian

{DAY}
19

# WHY DOES *THE NUTCRACKER* BALLET ENDURE?

When the curtain comes up on the opening scene of *The Nutcracker* ballet, we see a lovely living room lavishly decorated and filled with people in fancy clothes who are chatting, laughing, and dancing. Children skip and play in the festive room. The focal point is the beautiful fireplace mantle and a magnificent Christmas tree. Everything sparkles with Christmas colors. Red! Green! Silver! Gold! We see an equally beautiful scene in *The Nutcracker and Four Realms*, a 2018 film version that is loosely based on the original story.

But what always makes this opening scene so magical and memorable to me isn't the fancy clothes or the expensive presents, but the sense of community and hospitality. This Christmas Eve party is warm, welcoming, hospitable, and full of laughter and joy. As a child, I wanted to *be* at that party, to walk in the door and have someone's face light up and wave me over for a hug! These days, my husband and I do our best to recreate this scene at our annual Christmas party each year. Beyond the inspirational image of fellowship, the ballet also gives us the gift of beauty.

In 1892, Peter Tchaikovsky released his ballet *The Nutcracker Suite*, which was based on a story called "The Nutcracker and the Mouse King," written in the late 1700s by E. T. A. Hoffmann and tweaked by the well-known author Alexandre Dumas. But initial reviews of the ballet in Russia were poor. Incredibly, Tchaikovsky himself had been less than enthusiastic about working on it. Yet the average person loved it. The community delighted in the magic, wonder, extravagance, and beauty of the imaginative fairy tale and lush music. *The Nutcracker* soon found favor in other parts of the world, and came to America in 1944, where it has delighted audiences ever since.

{ DAY }
19

# Go See the Ballet That Says Christmas!

*This year, go enjoy your local community's performance of* The Nutcracker. *The beauty of the gorgeous spectacle creates long-lasting, magical memories. Many local ballet companies will adapt* The Nutcracker *to a certain time period or specific events. For example, in Nashville, Tennessee,* The Nutcracker *is set in 1897, the time of the Tennessee Centennial Exhibition, and the main ballroom is set in a local mansion. See what local flavor your own community ballet company will offer!*

{ DAY }

# 20

# Wreaths

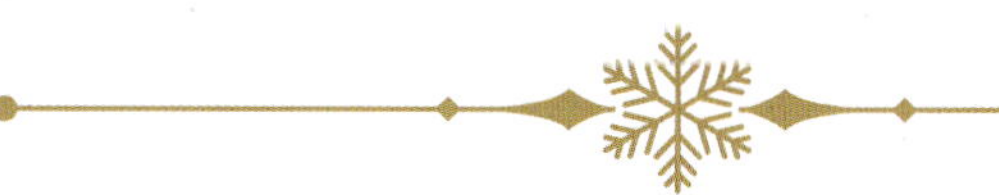

*Oh! Christmas wreath upon the wall,*
*Within thine ivied space*
*I see the years beyond recall,*
*Amid thy leaves I trace*
*The shadows of a happy past,*
*When all the world was bright,*
*And love its magic splendour cast*
*O'er morn and noon and night.*

–Anna de Brémont
"The Christmas Wreath"

{ DAY }
20

# WHAT DO WREATHS SYMBOLIZE?

I once observed a husband-and-wife team making wreaths at the Holiday Tree Farm outside Summerville, South Carolina. At first glance, it seemed so easy, filling the round metal circle with pieces of evergreen. But it is harder to do than it appears. Like anything, wreath-making is a skill that requires practice. But the final product, a staple of Christmastime, holds plenty of spiritual symbolism.

First, a wreath is a circle, and this reflects everlasting life in Jesus. The circle of a wreath also represents eternity, for it has no beginning and no end. Holly branches, which often are used in a wreath, represent the crown of thorns on Jesus's head when he was crucified. Finally, because the wreath is almost always hung on the doors of homes and churches, it stands as a beacon of hospitality. It's a signal that Christ is welcome in the homes, the communities, and the hearts of all who take such care to place it where everyone can see it. We're reminded to open our hearts and homes to each other—and to Jesus.

{ DAY }

20

# Craft Your Own Circle of Hope and Hospitality

*Have a wreath-making party, at home or*
*as a special project for families at church.*
*You'll need frames fashioned from wire or Styrofoam,*
*evergreens, bows, and whatever other decorations*
*suit the story of you and your family.*
*Hang your wreath on your front door*
*as a symbol of hospitality.*

# { DAY } 21

# *Gift-giving*

*"Where is the child who has been born king of the Jews? For we observed his star at its rising, and have come to pay him homage." . . . On entering the house, they saw the child with Mary his mother; and they knelt down and paid him homage. Then, opening their treasure chests, they offered him gifts of gold, frankincense, and myrrh.*

–Matthew 2:2, 11

{ DAY }

# 21

# IS GIFT-GIVING A RELIGIOUS OR SECULAR PRACTICE?

You probably remember that one Christmas gift that you just had to have when you were younger. Maybe it was a Cabbage Patch Kids doll, your first bike, or the latest Backstreet Boys CD (OK, I am seriously dating myself here!). These memories—the longing for something special, and the joy of receiving it—stay with us. But as I get older, the gifts that mean the most are priceless: good health, laughter, family nearby, life. And something else that changes as you get older is the realization that giving gifts is more enjoyable than getting gifts.

Giving each other gifts during Christmas is a direct reflection of the gifts the Three Wise Men brought to the baby Jesus. These gifts—gold, frankincense, and myrrh—carried profound significance in those times. The gold represented royalty, which was appropriate to herald the birth of the one true King. Frankincense represented Jesus's purity as a priest of God. And the myrrh foreshadowed his death, since myrrh was used as an anointing oil and for embalming.

Gift-giving also reminds us of the most important Christmas gift of all: Jesus. How can you honor the original intent of gift-giving in your presents this year? How can your gifts be meaningful to the people who will be receiving them? Homemade gifts can be enjoyable and fulfilling to make. Start a gift tradition that your family can be known for—like delivering a Christmas lasagna, or a platter of your own family-favorite Christmas cookies. A hand-knitted scarf or the promise of shoveling your elderly neighbor's sidewalk are priceless gifts sure to be treasured. Heartfelt, handwritten Christmas cards can warm hearts and help you stay in touch with loved ones who live out of town.

{ DAY }

# 21

# Reinvent Gift-Giving

*This holiday season, consider creating a more meaningful gift-giving tradition by simplifying. Some families choose to give just three gifts to each member, inspired by the three gifts brought by the wise men to the baby Jesus. To start, gather for a family discussion about ways to bring more intention into your holiday giving. Ask each person to share ideas on how to make the experience more memorable, whether by focusing on handmade gifts, acts of kindness, or special experiences instead of material items. The youngest voices might surprise you with their creativity and thoughtfulness! Together, you can create a tradition that emphasizes thoughtfulness, gratitude, and the true spirit of Christmas.*

# { DAY } 22

# Nativity Scene

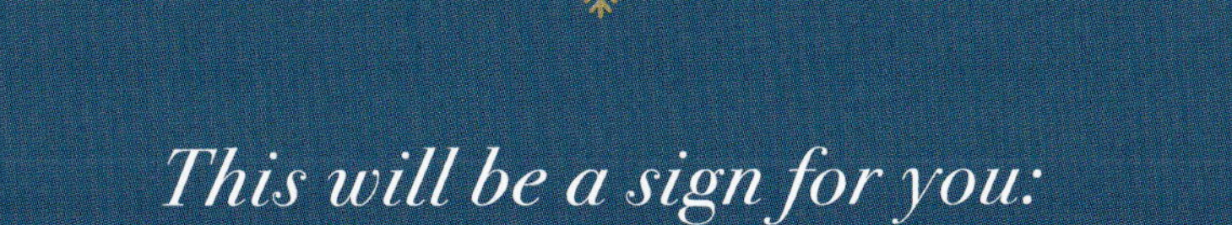

*This will be a sign for you:*
*you will find a child wrapped in bands*
*of cloth and lying in a manger.*

—Luke 2:12

{ DAY }

# 22

## WHO CREATED THE FIRST NATIVITY SCENE?

We see them displayed in homes, in churches, and on front lawns: the three-dimensional representations of the Christmas story we know as a nativity scene, or crèche. Mary, Joseph, baby Jesus, angels, shepherds and their sheep, the Three Wise Men, and stable animals are the cast of characters who assume their positions in and around the stable where Jesus was born. But where did the idea of the nativity come from?

Many believe that credit should be given to St. Francis of Assisi. In 1223, St. Francis is said to have built a wooden manger and created a display with live animals in a monastery in Greccio, Italy. Inspired by the time he had recently spent in the Holy Land, he did this to illustrate more widely the birth of Jesus as described in the Gospel of Luke. Perhaps because Jesus was born to a poor family, legend has it that St. Francis asked a poor family to participate in the scene, including the laying of their newborn baby in the manger. Townspeople assumed their places on the set as representatives of the other characters who figured in that holy night.

The birth of Jesus was not fancy; it was simple. But in this gift of simplicity, we find beauty, courage, humility, and strength.

{ DAY }

# 22

# Bring the Nativity Story to Life

*This Christmas, immerse your family in the story of Jesus's birth by finding or creating a beautifully arranged nativity scene on a lawn, and spend time reflecting on the true meaning of Christmas. If there's a drive-thru or walk-thru nativity at a nearby church, make an outing of it. Look for local community centers, parks, or shopping malls that feature a nativity. At home, create a special place where everyone can enjoy the nativity. Some families wait until Christmas morning to place the baby Jesus in the manger. End the day with a family movie night featuring* The Star, *a film that is a perfect reminder of the wonder and joy that is at the heart of Christmas.*

# {DAY} 23

# TRADITIONAL *Refreshments*

*Christmas is the season
for kindling the fire of hospitality
in the hall, the genial
flame of charity in the heart.*

—Washington Irving

{ DAY }
23

# WHAT'S THE TRADITIONAL HOT DRINK FOR CHRISTMAS EVE?

There seem to be two sets of people during the holidays: Team Hot Cocoa and Team Eggnog. As for me, you'll usually find me on Team Eggnog, so I was delighted to discover an eggnog recipe that is both easy to make and representative of the first Christmas. The oranges and orange zest in the eggnog can symbolize the gold brought by the first king to baby Jesus. The nutmeg represents the frankincense gifted to Jesus by the second king. The ground cinnamon or cinnamon stick represents the myrrh that was brought by the third king. Beyond the sweet taste of eggnog, I find it very comforting to hold a cup of golden symbolism during the holidays. Like a crackling fire and the beauty of softly falling snow, the gifts of comfort resonate with love and kindness.

{ DAY }
23

# Share a Cup of Christmas Cheer

*For my eggnog lovers, roll up your sleeves this Christmas Eve and make this delicious drink. (Don't worry, parents, this one is non-alcoholic!) Maybe have an eggnog taste test, with everyone weighing in on variations in the ingredients. What happens when we add vanilla? Chocolate? Or sprinkle allspice or pumpkin spice instead of nutmeg over the drink?*

*And if eggnog isn't your thing, try this festive drink: Grandma's Christmas Punch, which comes to you courtesy of Paula Hinckley and her family.*

{ DAY }

23

# GRANDMA'S CHRISTMAS PUNCH

*INGREDIENTS*

1 large can pineapple juice

2 packages Kool-Aid pink lemonade

1½ cups sugar

10 cups hot water (to dissolve sugar)

2 Tbs. almond extract pure flavoring

½ liter ginger ale

*DIRECTIONS*

Freeze the ingredients in a plastic container.

Remove from freezer about 1 hour before serving.
Chop up frozen mixture and put in punch bowl.
Add about ½ liter ginger ale to mixture.
Punch should be a slushy consistency.

Credit and gratitude to Paula Hinckley for sharing her recipe.
Thank you, Paula!

# CHRISTMAS EGGNOG

*INGREDIENTS*

1 quart of grocery store eggnog

1½ cups whole milk

1 16-ounce container frozen orange juice

ground nutmeg

orange zest from 1 orange

cinnamon sticks or ground cinnamon

*DIRECTIONS*

In a large pitcher, combine the eggnog, orange juice, and milk. Blend thoroughly. Refrigerate for several hours to give all the flavors time to combine.

Now it's time to zest your orange. Wash the outside of the orange. Using a fine cheese grater, grate the entire peel, getting all the good color off of the orange.

Use small clear glass cups (punch glasses are perfect) to serve so that the golden color of the orange eggnog can be admired.

Sprinkle each serving with orange zest and ground nutmeg, then either add a cinnamon stick or sprinkle with ground cinnamon.

Silent Night
Franz Xaver

# { DAY } 24

# "Silent Night"

*Silent Night! Holy Night!*
*All is calm, all is bright.*

—Lyrics by Joseph Mohr

{DAY}
24

a tempo
poco
the shepherds sing Glo-ry to our new born King; Peace, goodwill to men Peace
Silent Night, Holy Night!
Guiding Star shine ever bright
While the Eastern Magi bring
Gifts and homage to our King,
Peace, goodwill to men!

## WHY IS "SILENT NIGHT" SUCH A POPULAR CAROL?

To me, there is no more beautiful scene than a church aglow with candles as voices fill the sanctuary with the lyrics of the beloved Christmas carol "Silent Night." And this song has a rich history. An Austrian Roman Catholic priest named Joseph Mohr wrote the words in 1816, and the music was composed by Franz Xaver Gruber in 1818. The song was first performed on Christmas Eve in Austria, not long after the Napoleonic War, to lift the spirits of a country plagued by hunger, disease, and poverty.

The story goes that Joseph performed it that night with his guitar. Eventually, the song was translated into more than three hundred languages. Probably the most touchingly famous performance of the song happened during World War I. It was Christmas Eve, and the military leaders agreed to a temporary truce on the battlefield. The soldiers from both sides all began singing "Silent Night." That night, the lyrics were lifted up in three different languages: French, German, and English.

{ DAY }
# 24

# Cultivate Peace

*This year, when you hear "Silent Night," think of its message of peace and calm. Ask yourself: Is there anyone I need to seek peace with? Is there anyone I can call a truce with? We all can contribute in some small way to bringing to life the challenge of promoting peace embedded in these lyrics. On Christmas Eve, gather everyone together and listen to your favorite version—or maybe several different performances—of "Silent Night." And then just be quiet and still. See who can last the longest (an activity my little kids surprisingly love to participate in), and revel in the great presence of God that we find in silence. Knowing that the holidays can be noisy, it's good to take a few moments just to be quiet.*

# { DAY } 25

# *Sing* "HAPPY BIRTHDAY"

*To you is born this day in the city of David a Savior, who is the Messiah, the Lord.*

–Luke 2:11

{DAY}
25

# SHALL WE SING "HAPPY BIRTHDAY" ON CHRISTMAS DAY?

We made it! Merry Christmas, everyone! I hope these 25 days have enriched your life with more meaning and insight into what Christmas is all about. When we dig deep, we see that the Christmas season is rich in spiritual significance. And now, as we enjoy the glorious day that Christmas is, please join me in a tradition my family and I have just recently begun: we bake a birthday cake for Jesus. The act of baking or even just buying a birthday cake and putting candles on it, singing "Happy Birthday" to Jesus, and recognizing that today is our celebration of his birth puts things in perspective, especially for little ones. It is a great reminder that amid all the celebrations, decorations, and events of the day, the essential element is that this is the day Jesus was born into this world. So take a few minutes during your festivities to sing "Happy Birthday" to Jesus.

{DAY}
25

# Celebrate Merry Birthday

*This Christmas, make the holiday even more special by baking a birthday cake for Jesus as a family. Choose a favorite recipe or try a new one, letting everyone pitch in, from measuring the ingredients to mixing the batter to spreading and decorating the frosting. Once the cake is baked and frosted, add candles, gather around, and sing "Happy Birthday" to Jesus. Invite each family member to place a candle on the cake while sharing a hope for the coming year, or a prayer for a special intention. Consider inviting neighbors or friends to join in and share this heartfelt celebration that honors the true meaning of Christmas by bringing everyone together in love and gratitude.*

# A SPECIAL THANK YOU

Creating *The True Gifts of Christmas* has been a wonderful journey, and I am deeply grateful to the incredible team who made it possible.

Special thanks to publisher Joellyn Cicciarelli as well as Santiago Cortes, John Christensen, and Kim Skalman for their steadfast support.

To the dedicated marketing team—Carrie Freyer, Mary Alice Howard, Andrew Yankech, and Liz Emblem—your enthusiasm means the world. My heartfelt appreciation to Gary Jansen and Maura Poston for their editorial guidance and to Leanna Tankersley for her thoughtful editing.

A sincere thank you to the production and design team—Rob Ferry, Jill Arena, Carrie Schuler, Kathryn Seckman, Donna Antkowiak, Cepheus Edmondson, and Nikki Limper—for their creativity and hard work. Thanks also to Crane Giamo, Liz Lefebvre, and Bret Nicholaus for copyediting and proofreading.

Gratitude to Madeline Ramirez and Jody Yung for printing, and to Amber Williams, Lindsie Herring, and Kristy Belcher for their beautiful photography.

With love,

Megan

# ABOUT THE AUTHOR

Megan Alexander is an Emmy-nominated television host, executive producer, actress, and author. A recipient of both the coveted Telly Award for Hosting and the Cynopsis Award for Family Content, Megan is a national correspondent for the syndicated television show *Inside Edition*. She has covered *Thursday Night Football* on CBS and appears regularly on Fox News discussing issues of faith, family, and work. Megan is the author of *Faith in the Spotlight* and the Christopher Award–winning children's book *One More Hug*.

As a lover of all things Christmas, Megan has made it one of her life's goals to spread holiday cheer to all. She creates, produces, and hosts the television show *Small Town Christmas*, which airs on UPtv, and is the author of *The Magic of a Small Town Christmas*. She is a married mama of three young children and is active in her parish, St. Philip Catholic Church, in Nashville, Tennessee.

# ART ACKNOWLEDGMENTS

**Cover:** (t) Electric_Crayon/iStock/Getty Images; (c) Kristy Belcher; (bg) Anastasiia Krivenok/Moment/Getty Images; (b) MOMOKO SAKAI/iStock/Getty Images.

**Frontmatter:** **i**(t) Electric_Crayon/iStock/Getty Images; (bd) MOMOKO SAKAI/iStock/Getty Images; **iii** Ekaterina Romanova/iStock/Getty Images; Janis Abolins/Shutterstock.com; T. A. McKay/iStock/Getty Images; Becsteroony/DigitalVision Vectors/Getty Images. **iv** Lindsie Herring. **v** Electric_Crayon/iStock/Getty Images. **vi**(l) Courtesy of Megan Alexander. Photography by Amber Smith; (r) Nashville Ballet. **vii**(l) Lindsie Herring; (r) Lindsie Herring. **viii**(l) byanikona/500px/500px/Getty Images; (c) SergeiGorin/iStock/Getty Images; (r) Sanja Baljkas/Moment/Getty Images. **ix**(l) billberryphotography/iStock/Getty Images; (c) Anna Blazhuk/Moment/Getty Images; (r) ZU_09/DigitalVision Vectors/Getty Images. **x**(l) Troy Harrison/Moment/Getty Images; (c) CSA Images/CSA Images/Getty Images; (r) scisettialfio/iStock/Getty Images. **xi**(t) Dmytro Yashchuk/iStock/Getty Images; (c) SEAN GLADWELL/Moment/Getty Images; (r) bonniej/E+/Getty Images. **xii**(l) oksix/iStock/Getty Images; (r) Dynamic Graphics/liquidlibrary/Getty Images. **xiii**(l) Valengilda/iStock/Getty Images; (r) TokenPhoto/E+/Getty Images. **xiv**(l) valio84sl/iStock/Getty Images; (r) Svetlana-Cherruty/iStock/Getty Images. **xv**(l) Juanmonino/iStock/Getty Images; (c) Michael Burrell/iStock/Getty Images; (r) earleliason/E+/Getty Images. **xvi** Jobalou/DigitalVision/Getty Images. **xvii** yamasan/iStock/Getty Images.

**Interior:** **1** Muenz/iStock/Getty Images. **2** Tetiana Soares/iStock/Getty Images. **4**(tl) Elva Etienne/Moment/Getty Images; (tr) Sergey Mironov/Moment/Getty Images; (b) skynesher/E+/Getty Images. **5** MOMOKO SAKAI/iStock/Getty Images. **6** fcafotodigital/E+/Getty Images. **8**(tl) Vstock LLC/Vstock/Getty Images; (tr) Carol Yepes/Moment/Getty Images; (bl) Lindsie Herring; (br) mstahlphoto/E+/Getty Images. **10** Olga U/iStock/Getty Images. **12** Hybrid Images/Connect Images/Getty Images. **14**(t) GMVozd/E+/Getty Images; (bl) Lindsie Herring; (br) Gabriela Tulian/Moment/Getty Images. **16** Catherine Falls Commercial/Moment/Getty Images. **18** Ana Rocio Garcia Franco/Moment/Getty Images. **20** FatCamera/E+/Getty Images. **22**(t) 2ndLookGraphics/E+/Getty Images; (bl) Aleksandra Shamonina/iStock/Getty Images; (br) IzdatStock/Shutterstock.com. **24** Svetlana Khoroshilova/iStock/Getty Images. **26** Anna Blazhuk/Moment/Getty Images. **28** TriggerPhoto/E+/Getty Images. **30** FG Trade Latin/E+/Getty Images; Photo courtesy of Megan Alexander; 32 Lew Robertson/Stone/Getty Images; 13-Smile/iStock/Getty Images. **34** Provided under license from The Crosiers. **36** Comstock/Stockbyte/Getty Images. **38** krblokhin/iStock/Getty Images. **40** Tetra Images/Tetra Images/Getty Images. **42**(t) LittleCityLifestylePhotography/iStock/Getty Images; SimoneN/iStock/Getty Images. (bl) JGI/Jamie Grill/Tetra images/Getty Images; (br) Gpointstudio/Connect Images/Getty Images. **44** sedmak/iStock/Getty Images. **46** HelmaghiStock/Getty Images. **48** John W. Banagan/Stone/Getty Images. **50** Timofey Zadvornov/iStock/Getty Images. **52**(t) ScrappinStacy/iStock/Getty Images; (bl) eROMAZe/iStock/Getty Images; (br) Yuliya Starikova/iStock Editorial/Getty Images. **54** visualspace/E+/Getty Images. **56** marilyna/iStock/Getty Images. **58**(t) JohnnyGreig//E+/Getty Images; (bl) Andrew Fox/The Image Bank/Getty Images; (br) Photo courtesy of Megan Alexander. **60** Thomas Barwick/DigitalVision/Getty Images. **62** Olena_Z/iStock/Getty Images. **64**(t) Cavan Images/Cavan/Getty Images; (bl) fotograzia/Moment/Getty Images; (br) Grzegorz Jermołaj/iStock/Getty Images. **66** Cavan Images/Cavan/Getty Images. **68** Montse Cuesta/Moment/Getty Images; Viktoriya_Podgornaya/iStock/Getty Images. **70** justsolove/iStock/Getty Images. **72** RealCreation/iStock/Getty Images. **74** victoshafoto/iStock/Getty Images. **75** victoshafoto/iStock/Getty Images. **76** Anastasia Turshina/iStock/Getty Images. **78** YEVHEN ANZIN/iStock/Getty Images. **80** Carol Yepes/Moment/Getty Images. **82** Xsandra/E+/Getty Images. **84** Lindsie Herring; zdravinjo/iStock/Getty Images. **86**(t) Lindsie Herring; (b) Lindsie Herring; 88 borchee/iStock/Getty Images. **90** Dynamic Graphics/liquidlibrary/Getty Images. **91**(t) Dynamic Graphics/liquidlibrary/Getty Images; (b) Dynamic Graphics/liquidlibrary/Getty Images. **92**(tl) franckreporter/E+/Getty Images; (tr) Betsie Van Der Meer/Stone/Getty Images; (b) RyanJLane/E+/Getty Images. **94** PoppyPixels/iStock/Getty Images. **96** Wavetop/iStock/Getty Images. **98** ArtBoyMB/E+/Getty Images. **100** Jose Luis Pelaez/Stone/Getty Images. **102** Tom Merton/OJO Images/Getty Images. **104** Lindsie Herring. **106** Julius Reque/Moment/Getty Images. **108**(t) yul38885 yul38885/iStock/Getty Images; John Leech, Public domain, via Wikimedia Commons. PD-US-expired. (bl) CraigRJD/iStock/Getty Images; (br) Elly Schuurman/Moment/Getty Images. **110** evgenyatamanenko/iStock/Getty Images; Julius Reque/Moment/Getty Images. **112** Steve Hilchey/500px/Getty Images. **114** Jeff J Mitchell/Staff/Getty Images News/Getty Images. **116**(t) IGOR KOVALENKO/EPA-EFE/Shutterstock.com; (b) Alastair Muir/Shutterstock.com. **118** Tetra Images/Digital Vision/Getty Images. **120** Mike Brinson/The Image Bank/Getty Images. **122**(t) Kseniya Ovchinnikova/Moment/Getty Images; (bl) Catherine Delahaye/DigitalVision/Getty Images; (br) Lindsie Herring. **124** clodio/iStock/Getty Images. **126**(t) Maria Korneeva/Moment/Getty Images; (bl) brusinski/E+/Getty Images; (br) Sean Justice/The Image Bank/Getty Images. **128**(t) GMVozd/E+/Getty Images; (bl) Coolpicture/Moment/Getty Images; (br) NoDerog/iStock/Getty Images. **130** mazzo1982/iStock Editorial/Getty Images. **132**(t) Rebecca Nelson/The Image Bank/Getty Images; (br) Fred de Noyelle/Stone/Getty Images. **134** steverts/iStock/Getty Images. **136** Ulza/iStock/Getty Images. **138** monkeybusinessimages/iStock/Getty Images. **140**(tl) MurzikNata/iStock/Getty Images; (tr) GMVozd/E+/Getty Images; (b) fotostorm/E+/Getty Images. **142** Courtesy Megan Alexander; istetiana/iStock/Getty Images. **144** Jamie Grill Photography/Tetra images/Getty Images. **146**(tl) Paolo Paradiso/iStock Editorial/Getty Images; (tr) LiliGraphie/iStock/Getty Images; (b) DGLimages/iStock/Getty Images. **148**(t) sedmak/iStock/Getty Images; (bl) herpens/iStock/Getty Images; (br) Eriksson, Per/Johner Images Royalty-Free/Getty Images. **150** eclipse_images/E+/Getty Images. **152** yamasan/Creatas Video+/Getty Images. **154**(tl) Capelle.r/Moment/Getty Images; (tr) Natalia Lebedinskaia/Moment/Getty Images; Goodshoot/Getty Images; (b) Catherine Falls Commercial/Moment/Getty Images. **157** Lindsie Herring.